Level One Lean

Level One Lean

The Basic Problem Solving Tools and Mindset Required to Understand Lean

Kevin R. Wack

Copyright © 2011 by Kevin R. Wack
All rights reserved. No part of this publication may be reproduced, distributed, or transmitted in any form or by any means, including photocopying, recording, or other electronic or mechanical methods, without the prior written permission of the publisher, except in the case of brief quotations embodies in critical reviews and certain other noncommercial uses permitted by copyright law. For permission requests, write to the publisher, addressed "Attention: Permissions Coordinator," at the address below.

Box 641, Station Fort Langley
British Columbia Canada V1M 2S1

Ordering Information
Quantity sales. Special discounts are available on quantity purchases by corporations, associations, and others. For details, contact "wack01@telus.net".

Printed in the United States of America

Wack, Kevin (Kevin R.)
Level One Lean: The Basic Problem Solving Tools and Mindset Required to Understand Lean / Kevin R. Wack

Business & Economics / General

ISBN-13: 978-1466401860
ISBN-10: 1466401869

---

*To Linda and each of our wonderful kids,
you make life exciting and I'm grateful
to you for that.*

Contents

Introduction 13
Value 17
   What do you value? 21
The Eight Wastes 25
   The eight wastes 25
   1. **Motion** 31
      Where is your wasted motion? 35
   2. **Waiting** 37
      What Do You Wait For? 41
   3. **Transportation** 43
      When does the waste of transportation show up in your day? 47
   4. **Storage** 49
      Where do you have wasted storage in your day? 55
   5. **Defects** 57
      Who creates defects in your business? 61
   6. **Processing** 63
      Where do you overprocess? 65
   7. **Overproduction** 67
      Where do you overproduce? 69
   8. **Untapped People Potential** 71
      Why don't you tap all your People Potential? 73

Got your Lean Lenses on?

Spotting the Wastes 75

    Tips for Spotting Waste: 75

        Look for it! 75

    Necessary Waste 79

        Examples of necessary waste: 79

        Removing Waste 81

The Basic Lean Tools 83

    Kaizen 85

    5S 85

        So what is 5S? 87

    Sort 89

    Stabilize 95

    Shine 99

    Standardize 101

    Sustain 103

    Spaghetti Diagram 107

    Cycle Time Reduction 111

    Process Selection 115

    Step 1 117

    Step 2 119

    Step 3 121

    Step 4 123

    How should I personally use these tools? 129

Got your Lean Lenses on?

Employee Role	129
Personal Lean	137
The Two Minute Rule	137
Never go empty handed	139
Stop Doing List	139
Just Say No	141
Management Role	143
Set a 'True North' Direction	145
Deming's 14 points	145
Target Lean Activities for Leverage	149
Coaching & Developing Their People	151
Keeping things light	151
Focus on the process.	151
Problem solving mode	153
50% Process and 50% People	155
Bottom up and top down	157
Conclusion	161
Level One Lean Terms	162
Index	167
Acknowledgements	169

Got your Lean Lenses on?

Introduction

Most people have never heard of Lean, and until a few years ago it was mostly used in the manufacturing world, particularly in those companies that either supported or were wholly involved in making cars. This book doesn't have too much to do with cars; it's got more to do with sharing a basic level of knowledge about Lean. The intent is that it's a super practical easy to read book for those who aren't really interested in putting in ten thousand hours to learn it.

This book is for people who work at regular businesses, the kind that 98% of us work at. You know the kind; maybe they make tables or chairs, or help people declutter their homes prior to selling. At these regular businesses most often we spend our time doing our own thing being concerned about how our day is going, about the tasks we have to do and about what's going on with our coworkers. Often we don't even think about our customer.

Thankfully, at the core of Lean is the customer. When we've adopted the philosophy of Lean we really only want to do that which the paying customer is willing to pay for. Like making sure we've put a terrific paint finish on the car or achieved on time delivery. Of course, there are activities we all do that no customer wants to pay for (like paying for marketing) and one of the fun parts of Lean is learning to use a basic, easy to use set of tools to help minimize those activities.

I've been involved with Lean for a number of years; so long it seems I can barely recall what my life was like before Lean. I have long been pretty organized and thought I was efficient. Learning about Lean has helped me see things I thought true were not and some things I thought were not true indeed were. In the old days I used my intuition and gut as my data and facts, since learning Lean I've begun to learn how to use real data and facts. Sometimes gut and data match, sometimes they don't. Learning how to accept the data and fact over intuition, and then using intuition to accept and know its ok may be the biggest benefit I've gained.

Enjoy your Lean journey, take your time, and learn to learn deeply so you don't have to backtrack too much.

Kevin Wack, September 2011

How to use this book

This book is organized in the following manner: every second page has a brief statement describing the more detailed notes on the pages surrounding it. To help speed your understanding read the pages on the left; they will provide you with some thoughts and detail to learn about Lean to get a solid base of knowledge to begin from.

Value is defined as whatever the customer is willing to pay for.

Value

What is value?

Whatever the customer is willing to pay for.

That's it. Whatever the customer is willing to pay for, they value. Everything else in a business is waste, which we'll get to later. For now, just consider the mindset that value is whatever the customer is willing to pay for.

Customers decide what they value each time they spend money. When they head to a fast food shack for lunch, clearly they value speed over quality; when it's casual fine dining it may be that they value atmosphere over speed. Anyone who's hung out in a Starbucks for any length of time likely values that created, 'not by chance' European atmosphere.

So, value can be all kinds of things, in our Lean world here we'll stick to 'what the customer is willing to pay for'. What's great about this description is it helps focus the mind very quickly when looking at a system or process.

When we look at processes or systems, it really helps if we put on these amazing sunglasses (you know the kind, super stylish) that come with high tech lenses known as Lean lenses.

Got your Lean Lenses on?

2 Goals this book would like to help you with:

1. How to spot waste

2. How to remove waste

Got your Lean Lenses on?

As soon as I look at things through my Lean lenses, all sorts of things show up; 'I'd pay for that! Oh, I don't want to pay for that. Why do they do that? It seems no one really likes that...' As you learn about value and look around your business/home/activities you'll find all kinds of things you value, and all kinds of things you don't. With some luck, things you don't value are valued by someone (you may not be the targeted customer!) else.

We want to hone our Lean lenses so we can confirm that *what we think is happening is what is actually happening.*

When my wife brings my youngest daughter shopping, she likes to shop at every store and look at every outfit on every rack. She really values the mall experience and is therefore willing to pay for the entire infrastructure. When I go shopping, I want to be in and out with my items in minutes or less. I'm not interested in walking through the big mall with marble floors and I sure don't want to pay for it!! Maybe that's why malls all over North America are struggling? We've figured out there are specialty stores we can get in and out of, that have a terrific selection of products that are competitively priced and we don't have to walk two miles to get in and out of. Now that's value (for me anyway)!

When we shop for fruit and vegetables, my wife & I value when it won't be overripe the day we bring them

Got your Lean Lenses on?

The core of Lean is to only do what the (paying) customer is willing to pay for.

Doing this helps us provide maximum value to that customer.

home. Whole Foods has figured out many of their customers feel the same way. I've visited some manufacturers that haven't figured this stuff out. One that comes to mind is a food processor for both consumers and the restaurant and hospitality industry. This company did not realize that the restaurants and hotels who were their customers didn't really value the sixteen different containers this business used to pack their wares in. Their customers would likely have been happy with a few basic packages, but somewhere along the way this business got into carrying hundreds of thousands of containers, thinking their customers 'valued' the unique packaging. All they had to do was ask; we did and they told us they didn't care about the packaging. The customers valued the contents of that packaging. They needed it to work, to re-seal well, but that's it!

What do you value?

How do you know if you value something?

Consider where you spend your money. Why do you support these businesses? What is it about them that makes you shop there? Is it speed, ambience, convenience, quality? Take a few minutes and really think about it. Write down the reasons here on the page.

Grocery store, coffee shop, clothing store?

Lean is a philosophy that utilizes a set of problem solving tools that drive continuous improvement.

What are your hobbies? Do you shop at a Mom & Pop or a mega we have everything store?

Do you use government facilities like the local library or swimming pool? You're paying for them. Do you value them? How about the technology you use, do you use Google? Why?

Where did you buy your car? Some people like to buy at a 'one price for everyone' dealership while others prefer to negotiate with the leisure suit guy.

There are many reasons we 'value' the various businesses we shop at and the same is true for all businesses or places where 'stuff' happens.

Take the time to put on the Lean Lens sunglasses and practice studying what people value. Doing so really helps us see which wastes live in and around our places of work.

Got your Lean Lenses on?

Lean Lenses Sunglasses for sale!

Got your Lean Lenses on?

The Eight Wastes

The bedrock of Lean is these eight wastes. Originally there were seven, but somewhere along the way someone recognized that when one of the seven are present, the eighth automatically shows up, so it should be listed as well.

The eight wastes are important because once we learn how to spot them in their many forms; we can start to remove them which is the real goal of Lean, do only what the customer values, or, what they would be willing to pay for.

The eight wastes
1. Motion
2. Waiting
3. Transportation
4. Storage
5. Defects
6. Processing
7. Overproduction
8. Untapped People Potential

Shigeo Shingo of Toyota was the first person to recognize these wastes, or perhaps the first person to write them down. I doubt he knew as he described them to the people around him how much of an impact his list would make on generations of businesses and the people who work in them.

Got your Lean Lenses on?

Learn Lean in 12 words:

1. Forget title.
2. Go see.
3. What is the problem?
4. Go fix.
5. Go do.

Got your Lean Lenses on?

We'll look at these eight wastes one by one, with the goal of helping you be able to recognize when, how, and why they show up, then, we'll talk about what you can do about them when you find them. They live at work, at home, and in the businesses where you buy your clothes, music, and golf clubs. They're in government (rampant?), private business, not for profits. They're in my shop at home. Just everywhere.

How could that be? How could all these very successful businesses and institutions be rife with waste? The answer is pretty straightforward for me.

We just add things all the time. It's almost like the human condition is laid out to add; at work where we often add a step to a process, or we add a machine, or a forklift or another person, instead of figuring out how to add more value (what the customer is willing to pay for) with the same amount of resources or even fewer.

I did a project at a business where there was an experienced Sales Manager who had been in his role for a number of years. His customers, peers, and staff really liked him, a terrific guy. We'll call him Jim. Jim was an expert 'adder'. When we looked at the sales counter Jim was responsible for, we were shocked to see that over the years, he had 'added' so many steps to these peoples' jobs that when we removed all (or as much as we could) of the waste we could find during the one project, we were shocked to discover they had

Got your Lean Lenses on?

Lean is about bringing problems to the surface so we may think and work to fix or eliminate them.

Got your Lean Lenses on?

25% too many people in place to get the work done!

It was devastating. Here these extra people were doing work that they were told was important and were asked to do bits and pieces of every day. So they poured their soul into these tasks and suddenly we had to ask them to stop doing these things. Some lost their jobs. Some were asked to take jobs in different areas of the business. All because Jim thought he was doing the right thing by adding steps or processes that the customers weren't really interested in paying for. Jim didn't know he was adding waste. He thought he was doing the right thing by adding work. He didn't realize that the customers didn't want to pay for what he was adding.

Rather than being expert 'adders', we need to become expert removers of these wastes.

To help, let's go through them one at a time and look at how well they seem to group together like a pack of teens at the mall.

Got your Lean Lenses on?

The waste of motion includes all sorts of motion: walking, reaching, bending.

1. Motion

Ever walk out to your car parked at the far end of your driveway to get something only to discover it isn't there? Then, just as you close the door on your way back in you remember it's in your jacket pocket or purse? That's the waste of motion.

Unnecessary motion is when your wife drives to the mall four times in one weekend when one trip with a list would have sufficed. At work, I've watched people walk 160 feet to pick a document off a printer only to repeat that same walk 15 times in one day. With 5,280 feet in a mile, every one of these folks walk more than a half a mile *every day*! I'm not their customer specifically, but, if I were, I would absolutely not want to pay for them to get their exercise. The most advanced Lean factories design work so the workers' entire range of motion is inside a 48 inch circle surrounding them. Whoa! Quite a difference between 4 feet and 160 feet. The people in these factories can add a lot of value while the other folks are walking 156 feet.

The waste of motion is not just related to a single individual's work area, it also flourishes wherever groups work together. I toured a company recently that, like many, have grown organically over the years, taking the bay next to the original, then the next bay and so they currently rent four bays in their warehouse strip mall. If you've been in one of these warehouse

Got your Lean Lenses on?

The Eight Wastes:

1. Motion
2. Waiting
3. Transportation
4. Storage
5. Defects
6. Processing
7. Overproduction
8. Untapped People Potential

Got your Lean Lenses on?

strip malls you know what I'm talking about. The offices are stretched across four different buildings in a maze of stairwells and zigzags. I remember thinking if there was a fire I'd be in trouble because I was becoming lost in this maze. Watching these people work to communicate effectively with their peers was something else; you can already see it, can't you. The good news is after a relatively short time working at Lean, the ownership realized this and has made moves to reduce overall motion in the business and simply by relaying out the offices they've been able to release one of the bays, thereby saving themselves over $60,000 per year!

With the above examples of the waste of motion, you can see how the waste of untapped people potential creeps in as a result of the initial waste. This is true of all wastes. How can you have time to develop your potential if you're 'busy' walking half a mile a day to grab a document? Here's one of the challenges we find with many of the wastes: "it's 150 feet, what's the big deal, that's not much", yes, 150 feet isn't much, until you do some math; 150 ft X 5 people X an average of 5 times per day X 260 days per year = 184 miles. That's a long walk to grab a document (never mind the stops along the way). Why wouldn't you just move the printer to where the people are?

I love to look for waste wherever I go, and one business that is really well designed as far as a lack of motion

Got your Lean Lenses on?

Removing waste is easy; the hard part is spotting it.

Bruce Hamilton
GBMP – Greater Boston Manufacturing Partnership

Got your Lean Lenses on?

goes is Starbucks. Their baristas don't have to move too far to do their jobs. The cashier takes care of the order, writes your order onto the cup (they've been upgrading to reduce that motion by printing a label then sticking it onto the cup) and places it next to the barista who will make your order right where he stands. Once he makes your coffee he slides it onto the bar which is right next to him – nice workplace design!

A tougher workplace design might be the average mall shoe store. You've been in this one. You browse the shoes until you find a pair you're interested in, then, after you speak to the salesperson they go into the back, search around and then come back with your shoes to try on. That is wasted motion. Different shoe manufacturers have different sizings or fits as well, so when the size nine you asked for is too tight, off they go again to find a larger size for you to try. Heavy wasted motion. Some shoe stores have all the key sizes right where the displays are, so for 80% of their customers, they don't need the salespeople to walk back and forth, so they don't pay for that wasted motion.

Where is your wasted motion?
Where is there wasted motion in your day?

Do you have excess motion in your plant?

Do your salespeople travel across the country for unprofitable sales?

Got your Lean Lenses on?

Reducing waste makes business easier.

Got your Lean Lenses on?

2. Waiting

Someone a long time ago told me that procrastination is the art of keeping up with yesterday.

As I write this I'm waiting for my son Daniel to fulfill some commitments to help his mom out at our church. And I'm waiting and writing, so that's not a waste.

Most of us have been in a meeting situation where the meeting is being held up and there will be fifteen participants waiting for the meeting chair to begin, but he's on a call or simply running late (of course there's a good reason!). Every single minute that clicks over is actually 15 (15 participants X one minute = 15 minutes). *Ten minutes late is one hundred and fifty minutes. Most of us can get quite a bit done in one hundred and fifty minutes!* I absolutely adore the folks that run their meetings like a military boot camp. On time to start, on time to end.

At a food processing business we worked in, we watched an expensive piece of stainless steel equipment and its operators wait for the inbound pallet to be delivered so they could pour its contents into the machine to process. We watched the operators wait for quite some time. At about the twenty minute mark we could see the people getting upset because we were 'watching them work' and they weren't. They were waiting. Of course, one of the operators had enough and walked in the direction of the warehouse to see if

Got your Lean Lenses on?

Waiting comes in many forms: waiting for information, a phone call, parts, raw materials... the list is endless!

he could help (?) the forklift operator find the pallet. And we waited. Close to thirty-five minutes after the material was supposed to be there it arrived but now the operator who went off on the search and rescue mission wasn't there to feed the machine. A quick scan of the clock said it was lunch time so the two waiting at the machine center knew where to head, the lunch room. "We start up at 12:30 after lunch, see you then". We'd been at this machine for almost an hour and nothing had happened (unfortunately it was four people X one hour, that's four hours wasted!). That's one example of the waste of waiting!

You've probably lived this one. A customer sends in an order with 'almost' all of the information on the purchase order. We e-mail or call them for the rest of the info so we can process their order. Sometimes we get a hold of them right away, sometimes it's a glorious game of phone tag that really can't be overstated – how about four phone calls back and forth and maybe a day goes by before we can begin to process the order?

That's the waste of waiting popping up and smacking us again and again.

Waiting comes in many forms; it could be waiting for information, for a person, or even waiting for material from a supplier. Waiting literally means anytime we have to wait for something before we can do what we need to do before we push that work to the next step,

Got your Lean Lenses on?

Imagine if you never had to wait, if everything you needed to do your job was always there, at exactly the right time!

Got your Lean Lenses on?

be it to the external customer or the internal customer.

What Do You Wait For?

In your day to day life, what sorts of things do you wait for?

Information from your customer, your co-workers, boss?

In an airport, to go through security?

A taxicab, or perhaps public transit?

It takes 10 times as long to fix an error as it does to do the task the first time correctly.

Got your Lean Lenses on?

3. Transportation

With transportation as the header, you probably thought about my co-workers that we talked about earlier, walking to the printer, transporting that paper. You could say that was transportation not motion. That's what we find with wastes. They often bump up against and into each other while they weave over top and underneath each other.

This is why we want to make spotting waste our primary goal as we learn about Lean because it's easy to remove the waste, once we *spot* it!

Picture a forklift moving from one side of a warehouse to the other, travelling east to west with a big pallet on the forks. After the driver places the pallet down, he travels to the opposite side of the warehouse and repeats many, many times in a day. But he always travels west to east with nothing on the forks? Surely something has to make it back?

When we redesign warehouses we spend a number of hours following the various workers around, not to spy on them or see what they're doing wrong, but to doodle where they go on a line drawing map of the facility just so we can see what is really happening in the business! What we often find is the example of the forklift above happens hundreds of times in a single day. Unfortunately, when we do the math, 550' X 28 trips/hour X 8 hours/day X 3 forklift drivers = 369,600'

Got your Lean Lenses on?

Working with Lean is delicious because there are so many layers. Every time I think I've got it figured out another deeper meaning shows up.

(*70 miles*) the numbers are huge. When we talk with the forklift drivers described here, they aren't really surprised. They often don't realize that they could do anything about eliminating waste or that anyone even cared!

When we do the work to reduce the transportation waste we've found we can often reduce it by more than 20%, simply by redesigning the layout!

I will always remember travelling with a sales rep and him explaining to me how busy he was, how he was pinched for time, couldn't see all of his customers, you name it. When we got to a particular box store to make his call, we parked and headed in to see our customer. Part way through the call we walked back out to the car to get some display cleaning supplies, went back inside to clean the displays, then walked back out to the car to dump the cleaning supplies and pick up brochures. We went back inside to deliver the brochures up and down the aisles we had just been up and down three times. Really. I wish I was exaggerating.

The best part for me was the fellow I was with could not see what was happening, though hopefully you are beginning to! When we had our wrap up at the end of the day he was genuinely surprised when I pointed out how much available time he had had he not transported himself over and over the same tracks all throughout the day. He hadn't learned to spot waste yet, never mind figure out how to remove it. The good news for

The waste of transportation includes hauling products unnecessarily across a warehouse, a city, a state, or even a country.

Got your Lean Lenses on?

him was the next time I travelled with him he wasn't as scattered, he thought ahead and made adjustments so he could reduce the waste of transportation in his job and be more effective. The sales game is difficult enough when things go well; it's really hard when we 'waste' the days away.

Transporting product further than it needs to go, many trips to the grocery store, these are examples of transportation waste. Truckers are masters at eliminating this waste as they have to work hard for backhauls; often their only profit exists in a backhaul. Now if they could only unload their trucks themselves in the blink of an eye, they could remove the waste of waiting...

When does the waste of transportation show up in your day?

Do you make several trips to the back of the plant each day?

How many times do you walk down the hall for something that's really of low value?

Do you book meetings ad hoc or do you come up with a strategic plan to do them back to back, minimizing overall travel?

Got your Lean Lenses on?

Storing too much inventory or inventory of the wrong type is wasteful.

Buying too much of anything is a waste!

4. Storage

How could storage be a waste? We have inventory. We need to store it. Don't we? Yes. What about our files? We need to store those don't we? Yes. How about our marketing materials? Yes. I'm not suggesting we don't need to store them but perhaps *it's how* we store them or *how many* we store or *where we* store them.

I was in a business recently which handles large volumes of special orders that get shipped out in groups of packages. So they receive a few pallets of (lets use six as the example) material, break it down and then ship it out in, say, half pallet quantities. So they store the material as it waits for their customer to call and say, "Go ahead and ship the next batch". There's an amazing amount of waste in that little process. After they receive the initial six pallets, they'll pull off the first order and then put the pallets wherever there is space. Keep in mind this is happening in a space of about 10,000 sq ft, and it resembles a bit of a junk yard. There's 'stuff' everywhere. The pallets get put away wherever there's space and are forgotten about until the next order comes for another half pallet. Only now they don't know where those pallets were put. Let the searching begin!

So you can see what's happening here, can't you? John is searching (waste of motion) while Paul is waiting (waste of waiting) for the order. The wastes stack up on top of each other. Twenty minutes later we've found

Got your Lean Lenses on?

Existing systems produce existing results.
If something different is required, the system must be changed.

Sir Christopher Ball
More Means Different

the pallets and have dug them out and started to pick Paul's order which takes a few minutes and we're rushing so perhaps John makes a mistake (uh oh). We're lucky today because he hasn't made a mistake. So let's tally some waste; 20 minutes each for John and Paul tallies up to only 40 minutes of waste. But John isn't the forklift driver digging for the pallets, so we have to add the 20 it took for Barry to pull out the pallets, then to be fair we should add the 10 minutes it took for John to pull the order once the pallets were in the open. 10 more for Paul waiting for the picking and we've got 80 minutes!

Surely that can't be right. But it is right. One order, in one business in one industry. And there are hundreds of thousands of businesses!

As you can see there's a bit of waste around.

Imagine if storage was done well here. John receives the request to ship the next batch, he gets the forklift driver to pull 'those six pallets out' and the driver immediately drops them at John's workstation so he can get to work on them so the order is ready before Paul shows up to pick up his order. Ten minutes later, Paul arrives for his order, he gets loaded immediately and once Barry's completed loading Paul's truck he replaces the now lighter pallets back in the right spot, awaiting the next order. Customer gets what he wants in a timely fashion, doesn't hang around waiting for his

When working at reducing the wastes, it's worthwhile to do the math to discover what kind of savings you are creating!

supplier to deal with their storage (waste) issues and is super happy because they didn't slow him down in any way! So the time to build this order is 30 minutes, saving 50 minutes.

50 minutes is a huge savings, especially when you think that its 50 minutes times one order. How about 50 minutes X 20 orders X 260 business days? That's 24 months worth of wasted man hours that has been eliminated per year! Unfortunately, check the math, it's correct. Multiply that time by a wage and its big money. Sometimes I like to multiply that cost savings by three or four years just to illustrate how big the savings really are... The example we just used will either cost this business an extra $65,000 over two years or will save them $65,000 over two years and the best part is they get to decide which it will be!

You can likely think of many examples of wasted storage: closets overfilled with clothes we don't wear while we wait to 'slim down', products purchased with the hope of one day 'getting into that hobby'. Keeping obsolete material in inventory instead of writing it down (or off) to keep the books looking better; any accountant will tell you you're not fooling anyone thinking the seven year old inventory is still saleable, 'someone will buy it!' Maybe, but you probably shouldn't count on it!

Got your Lean Lenses on?

Saving 50 minutes times 20 orders times 260 business days times $18 per hour equals $78,000!

50 X 20 X 260 X $18/hr = $78,000

Savings like that makes it worth it to remove the waste, doesn't it?

Got your Lean Lenses on?

Where do you have wasted storage in your day?

How many hours of inventory do you carry in your business?

Do you buy so much 'stuff' you can't possibly use it inside of a two or three week window? How much is enough?

Are your products stored in the right location?

Do people have to travel extra distance just to access where products are stored? (Do you see how the wastes stack onto each other?)

Got your Lean Lenses on?

For many things, it takes just as long to do incorrectly as correctly.

Got your Lean Lenses on?

5. Defects

Defects are a self explanatory waste. If you make it wrong, it's waste! Or junk. Maybe both. Of course, like everything with Lean, or life, it's really not that simple. If you consider where in a process the defect is created, it can either be something that's no big deal or a really big waste that costs you or your company up to thousands of dollars, maybe more.

Anything I might produce and then pass to you and it doesn't work, that would be a defect. Maybe it's an air bubble in a piece of glass, a tear in a brand new carpet, or a couple of pieces of wood you've glued together incorrectly. These are all defects.

A friend of mine took a class and part of the deliverables for his class was to create a business, a product, and then sell the product to make as much money as he could over three months to donate to charity. I wanted to support my friend, so I purchased what I thought was a terrific product; it was a spreadsheet that made it easy to write up an SOP (standard operating procedure), I think they called it 'SOP123'. I paid my $100 and was excited to get the disc and create some SOP's (the previous way we did them was very labor intensive and frankly, a pain). I loaded the software, went to make it go, and ...nothing.

Pure defect.

Got your Lean Lenses on?

As individuals, we must make it a priority to not pass poor quality work to the next person in our process.

The person who sold it to me said the product was terrific, 'unbelievable', so I knew something had to be wrong with me. When I called, I got the 'uh, yeah, really? Let me check with my guy and I'll come back to you'. As you might guess, I'm still waiting for that call. Well, not really, but when he called he gave me the 'no you can't have a refund program'.

Pure defect.

So, this is what a defect looks and feels like. Not so good. Defects are an interesting waste for many reasons, the foremost being they can best be determined to be defects by the customer. Some glass manufacturers put labels on their glass that say 'small air bubbles are a natural part of this piece of glass and are not considered warranty-able items, they add to the richness of the piece of glass'.

Sure, it's a nice spin, but as the customer I view that bubble as a defect!

Sometimes people will pass on a defect in a process at work either knowingly or unknowingly and more value gets added to the item along the way, only to discover the defect down the road. One that immediately pops to mind is the O-ring that ultimately caused the space shuttle Columbia and her seven astronauts to perish.

The defect was in the design. Unfortunately, it was then manufactured to that flawed design, then passed on to the next step, and so on and so on, right up until the

Got your Lean Lenses on?

Defects pile on:

'The **Presidential Commission on the Space Shuttle *Challenger* Accident**, also known as the Rogers Commission (after its chairman), was formed to investigate the disaster. The commission worked for several months and published a report of its findings. It found that the *Challenger* accident was caused by a failure in the O-rings sealing a joint on the right solid rocket booster, which allowed pressurized hot gases and eventually flame to "blow by" the O-ring and make contact with the adjacent external tank, causing structural failure. The failure of the O-rings was attributed to a faulty design, whose performance could be too easily compromised by factors including the low temperature on the day of launch.'

Wikipedia

Got your Lean Lenses on?

ship disintegrated. Most defects aren't as big or dramatic as that O-ring design, but you can see how they can build on each other.

In the Lean world, we want to prevent defects from happening at all and we especially want to prevent passing defects on to someone else who adds more value to our defect then passes that item on.

Who creates defects in your business?
Do you knowingly create defects?

What do your co-workers do when they find a defect?

How do you define a defect? Something the customer says is a defect, or something you say is a defect?

Where in your value stream are defects created? Is it consistent?

Got your Lean Lenses on?

For many things, it takes just as long to do correctly as incorrectly.

Got your Lean Lenses on?

6. Processing

It's easy to understand how most of the wastes are indeed wastes. Walking hundreds of extra feet to pick up a wrench many times a day is clearly wasteful. As is sitting somewhere doing nothing while waiting for a co-worker to provide you with information you need to do your portion of the job.

But how is processing a waste? The job needs to be done. The machine needs to be built. How can that possibly be a waste? Processing is a waste (also known as inappropriate processing) which occurs when we have steps in a process that add no value. For example, if we assemble a part, take it apart and then reassemble for final assembly that is the waste of processing. Why not just assemble one time? Why do we have to take it apart? It makes no sense does it?

We really have to work hard to ensure the processing we do is done with a minimum amount of effort and that things are touched only once if at all possible.

A friend of mine has a small manufacturing company that punches sheet metal. They make millions of blanks every year. The first time we worked in her business we found an operator who had a job cleaning up the edges of these punched wafers of metal. This operator was placed in a small room just a few feet away from the loud thump of the metal punching machine. The folks

Got your Lean Lenses on?

There are no experts, just people with more experience.

The longer we wait, the more experience our competitors will have when we start.

John Shook
As Quoted in 'Becoming Lean'

Got your Lean Lenses on?

in this business discovered as they targeted removing processing waste, if they just punched the metal in a slightly different way, the operator would not have to polish off burrs for hours on end.

What did they do? They determined that if they maintained their punch press dies more frequently, pretty easy to do, they could use this operator's time to add more value elsewhere in the processing.

Where do you overprocess?
Do you handle e-mails three & four times before dealing with them?

Do you have an organized filing system in your computer or do you have to search for lost files?

When processing in your shop, do you have to go back to the same assembly station multiple times or do you assemble in one process?

Overproduction is the worst waste of the first seven because when overproduction happens, all the other wastes are created.

Got your Lean Lenses on?

7. Overproduction

When I was growing up in business I worked at a company that manufactured insulation, it was common for us to make more of certain types of insulation so we could 'get ahead'.

No one told us that overproduction was bad. Upper management likely thought it was a good thing we were 'getting ahead', otherwise they would have told us to stop. Too bad because often when we overproduced type A we would get an order for type B and we'd have to spend time (money) moving all the product A we had prebuilt. Sometimes we'd have to move it multiple times and we'd trip over product C we'd prebuilt and the discontinued product D that we prebuilt but no one bought anymore. This is a bit of an exaggeration, but not much and you get the idea!

If I was an accountant I'd talk about overproduction being bad for financial reasons because when we overproduce we create inventory and inventory costs money. How much money? Accountants generally use a number of 2% per month, which means if you overproduce $1,000 dollars of extra inventory that stack of product costs your business about $20 every month it sits unsold. Sure, $20 isn't that much, but when you do the math, and we have to do the math (here's a small example - $20 X 50 thousand dollars of excess inventory X 12 months = $12,000!), the numbers add up very quickly into real money. It should always be our

Got your Lean Lenses on?

'Why are you not making more progress? I don't understand...'

David Chao
Founder, Lean Sensei International

From an early coaching conversation with my sensei (coach), a gentle reminder of the need to think harder.

Got your Lean Lenses on?

goal to produce exactly what the customer wants, in exactly the quantity the customer requires. Overproduction is the worst of all the wastes because it always causes a number of the other wastes to be created. When we made too much of insulation type A we had to later move it, we had to store it, then we had to move it back to where it was in the first place!

Where do you overproduce?

Could you imagine overfilling your gas tank by a gallon every time you fill up?

Do you cook for six when there are only four people at your table?

Do you buy three weeks worth of meat when you go to Costco and then throw away half of it?

Got your Lean Lenses on?

CEO's dream for GE:
"I hope it will be the greatest learning institution in the world."

Jack Welch
Quoted by Robert Slater in
Jack Welch and the GE Way

Got your Lean Lenses on?

8. Untapped People Potential

Every time we create any of the first seven wastes, this waste appears. This waste was not on Shigeo Shingo's original list of wastes but has been added over time because it's a real and costly waste.

Whenever people do the wrong work or are producing something the customer doesn't value, we are underutilizing someone's talent or potential.

Every person wants to do a good job and we all want to do what is right for our customer. We can't do those things if we're working at something that is wasteful or no one wants to pay for. Whenever we were overproducing insulation Type A, we weren't providing what our customer wanted. We were wasting our talents building Type A. We could have been doing things the customer valued, like producing Type B, or experimenting to create Type G, which the customer *really* wanted!

There are other ways this waste shows up that aren't very good. For example, say I love to sell but my manager wants me to do something else, maybe build displays because I'm good at that too. My selling skills get wasted doing something simply because I'm good at something else, maybe I'm great at process management but because we need someone in assembly, my boss keeps me in assembly. S/he doesn't

When storing tools, only keep those used regularly on the shadowboard.

get the full value of my work or realize that perhaps I can save 20% in the assembly process simply by putting my talents to work there.

Not utilizing the talents of people around us is an extremely common way this waste shows up, particularly in those that are self-centered or internally motivated.

Why don't you tap all your People Potential?
Are you caught in the 'this is the way we've always done it' mentality?

Do you think you know the best way?

Do you work on things that aren't important?

Got your Lean Lenses on?

5S is a beautiful way to keep your mind free for doing work that really matters, like thinking and solving problems.

Got your Lean Lenses on?

Spotting the Wastes

So now that we know what the eight wastes are, we want to learn how to spot them so we can begin to strategically remove them, like a surgeon takes out cancer, first in the high risk areas, then, the areas that aren't as dangerous (as though cancer wouldn't be dangerous anywhere...).

It is a challenge for most of us as we are learning to spot waste, because it isn't easy to spot. Not that you can't see it, it's more that because it's so common in every business and work area that it's challenging to spot.

Tips for Spotting Waste:

Look for it!
Most people have been to a seminar or class where the facilitator has you look around the room, "look at everything you can see that is green, look hard around the room, find all the green, notice the Starbucks cups, look look look, now CLOSE YOUR EYES!; and tell me everything that is brown!" The entire audience groans. We know it's coming but we're so used to looking for what we want to see we forget to look at everything else. It's the same with waste.

Got your Lean Lenses on?

Make things visual:

Big, colorful storyboards draw people in...

Got your Lean Lenses on?

Later today or tomorrow, whenever you're at a business or at your work, look more slowly, scan your eyes from the floor up, left to right, right to left. Watch what is happening………. s l o w l y………., watch the people and ask yourself, 'are they adding value right now? If I am the customer, would I be willing to pay for what s/he is doing right now?'

Be a waste detective. 'Just the waste, ma am'. Look for things like the waiter walking back and forth with dishes rather than utilizing the trays that every restaurant has beside the kitchen. Look for mechanics walking back and forth to their tool boxes; does the tool box really have to be forty feet from my car? I'm paying $90 per hour and he's walking back and forth, back and forth… You might have someone put you on hold for five or six minutes, that's pure waste. Phone tag is waste too, isn't it? When companies write up a purchase order and put the wrong price on it, then e-mail it to their supplier, that's a waste too.

Spend time over the next few days teaching yourself to spot waste. It's really worth your investment because you will begin to become skilled at it, which is your real goal.

Got your Lean Lenses on?

Keep it clean:

NO unnecessary items
NO mess
NO dirt

Got your Lean Lenses on?

Necessary Waste

There are things we all do in our day to day jobs that we must do but that the customer would not be willing to pay for and could really care less whether we did or not. But the accountants care (because the government cares!) or management cares or the safety officer cares. We call these things necessary waste.

Examples of necessary waste:

Necessary waste is also prevalent throughout our organizations. An example of necessary waste might be financial reporting. Accounting or finance departments are legally required to produce financial statements, but you might agree that most customers don't really want to pay for that. Other examples might be double checking an order before it ships. A customer might not want to pay for it but a business may believe it's necessary. Why not pick the order correctly the first time?

As you are becoming a skilled waste spotter, see if you can separate the two as you're spotting. Is that a necessary waste that person is doing or just a pure waste that could/should be eliminated altogether?

When touring a facility -

Can you see the flow?

Can you see the pull?

Can you see the rhythm (takt)?

Got your Lean Lenses on?

Removing Waste

As I've said, the most difficult part of Lean is spotting waste because it is prevalent throughout our lives, in our homes and businesses.

The most important part of Lean is not spotting the waste; it's the removal of the waste you've found. The ideal state would be that we all spend some time each and every day removing the waste around us, in all areas of our lives. There is always waste to remove, so don't worry that you'll run out! At a Yamaha motorcycle factory I toured, 100% of the employees spend at least one hour per week working on removing waste and finding more ways to add value.

Our goal should be to remove all of the waste we spot, a lofty goal for sure, but one that we should strive to meet.

Got your Lean Lenses on?

When touring a facility look for *Disqoh!*

Delivery – is the system clear?

Inventory – is it the right amount?

Safety – is there a robust program?

Quality – is quality a priority?

Operating

    Cost – is lowering costs a priority?

Huddles – are huddles happening?

Andrew McFadyen
Ex-Toyota Executive
Lean Sensei International

Got your Lean Lenses on?

The Basic Lean Tools

North American 5S

1: Sort
2: Stabilize
3: Shine
4: Standardize
5: Sustain

Got your Lean Lenses on?

Kaizen

The Japanese word Kaizen means small improvement for the better. As you work through the various tools you will quickly see most possible improvements are small, but when you stack them on top of each other they become very large. This is Kaizen.

A common practice within Lean companies is to select a project and assemble a group of people to perform a Kaizen Blitz. A Kaizen Blitz is simply a blitz on the project with these people performing many small improvements on the problem, process, or work area.

Possibly the most powerful tool of all is a Kaizen mindset. Those willing to adopt a Kaizen mindset will find Lean very natural, because things can always be improved!

5S

Doing 5S makes everyone's work easier. When we have our tools nearby, whether they be pen, computer, a set of chisels or whatever, it means we can do 'the stuff' we want to do (the stuff that adds value), rather than searching or digging around for tools. 5S is a beautiful way to keep your mind free for doing work that really matters, like thinking and solving problems.

Japanese 5S

1: **Seiri** (Clearing up)

2: **Seiton** (Organizing)

3: **Seiso** (Cleaning)

4: **Seiketsu** (Standardizing)

5: **Shitsuke** (Training & Discipline)

So what is 5S?

5S is as much a mindset as anything else. Is it simply a way to 'keep a work area clean' as many people think? No, as you will discover as you progress in the Lean world there are many, many layers.

There are Five steps (surprise!) to 5S – Sort, Stabilize, Shine, Standardize, and what's always the hardest S, Sustain.

1. **Sort**
2. **Stabilize**
3. **Shine**
4. **Standardize**
5. **Sustain**

We begin using 5S by selecting the work area we're going to 5S. It's probably not realistic to say, "I'm going to 5S my warehouse" on the first try. With 5S we want to decide on an area (picking our project scope) we can tackle in a day or two. Avoid the 'three week project' for 5S – simply too much of an elephant for a bite at a time. Target a scope you can eat in a day or two. Any more than that and you'll run out of steam.

So we begin our 5S.

Got your Lean Lenses on?

During 5S

Throw away with courage!

Got your Lean Lenses on?

Sort

To sort we simply work our way through the entire workstation and sort through what's there. In our 5S we'll use common areas for many businesses and homes. Our business example will be the 'merchandising room' and our home example will be my shop (because it's the only room in my house that I really control!).

First, we pull out all the items that don't make sense to be there, including anything that isn't (really) used regularly.

In our merchandising room, we're going to pull out the brochures from 2002. 2003. 2004. Any brochure or marketing piece that hasn't been placed in a customer's hands in the last 24 months is out out out! We'll also remove the 'custom brochure holders' we had made in 1996. Why did we order 400 (@$17.40 each) when we only had 80 customers who would really use them?

I like to do projects in my shop. I have learned that to keep it clean I must 5S on a regular basis, so I've created a space to 'sort' on an ongoing basis. You may have this space in your garage or shop as well. In my shop it's the space between the two overhead doors, I use this area to place items that I know won't make it past the next trip to the waste transfer station (dump). It could be obsolete paint or stain, wood that won't be used in future projects, or motorcycle parts that will never be mounted on a motorcycle again. Recently I got

Got your Lean Lenses on?

1: Sort

Remove all items from the area; keep only those that are used regularly. Regularly means in the past two weeks, but better yet, daily.

Place items that haven't been used in weeks or months into a single area (Red Tag area) where it will be auctioned off to the group.

Some items will be taken, others will end up in the trash.

Got your Lean Lenses on?

rid of a front brake caliper from an old Kawasaki. I've never owned a Kawasaki in my life, but I held onto that part for three years, adding clutter and slowing down my useful search time.

What to do with Sorted material?
- **Throw out**
- **Red Tag**
- **Put back where it belongs**

Throw out with courage during a 5S. I spent some time with a business owner recently that couldn't bring herself to throw anything out. The business essentially had an extra 4000 sq feet of space rented for obsolete 'we're never gonna use that!' stuff. Expensive.

For fun I like to think of dollars over five year time periods. Doing so helps amp up the positives and is like a punch in the throat on the negative side. So here's the punch. She paid $121,000 (REAL MONEY) to hold onto stuff no one wanted.

Red Tag is for items we think that *someone* wants. It might be the maintenance person's or someone from accounting or administration. In our merchandising room we found a case of acetates that are used regularly in the business, they'd just been put in the wrong spot. So we returned them to the office supply cabinet. It was the same with the postage weigh scale, 'how did this ever end up here?'

Got your Lean Lenses on?

Red Tag Rule:

If it won't be used in the next 45 days, it gets a tag!

Red Tag anything that is borderline, you can always pull it back in later!

Got your Lean Lenses on?

Once we've completed all the 'red tagging' we'll hold an auction for the pile of things we weren't sure of, 'I don't want to throw it away, but I don't know where it goes'. We might leave this in a shared area so all the supervisors can peruse and we don't throw away something we shouldn't. As well, we want others to feel they've had their say. We want them to see the progress we made in the area.

In my shop when I 5S, I put stuff back where it belongs, all the coffee cups I've pulled from the kitchen, various books I've brought out there to read when I don't want to do anything but hang out in front of the fire.

Got your Lean Lenses on?

A Shadowboard done well has only the tools used regularly at the workstation.

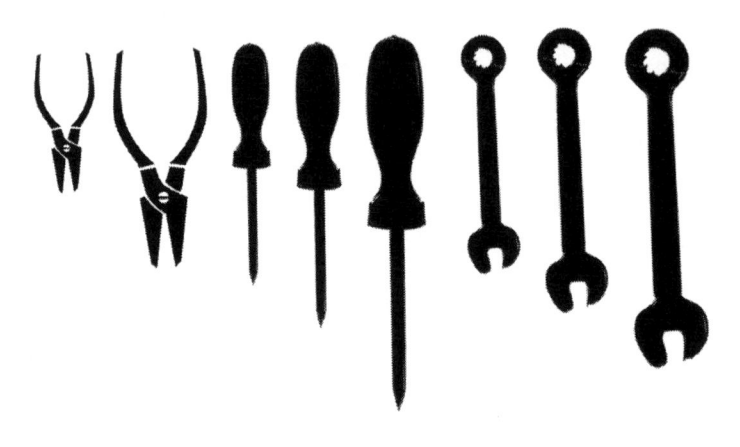

Here you see only three screwdrivers and three wrenches because that is what is required.

Extra tools create waste!

Got your Lean Lenses on?

Stabilize

A place for everything and everything in its place.

When we do a good job stabilizing, this is what we've done; we've got a spot for everything and everything is in that place. And 'that place' helps make the various tasks being done easier.

Whenever I fill one of my motorcycles with fuel after a ride, I need to add fuel stabilizer because who knows when I can ride again? Before I had 5S'd my shop, I kept this stabilizer with the other fluids on the far side of my shop so I'd have to (at times) climb over stuff, zigzag etc. to grab that container. Then I 5S'd! Now, it's on a small shelf with the few different cans/jars of fluids required to support proper maintenance of these bikes. Never more than five feet from where I ride in, it makes it very easy to keep my bikes maintained. Additionally, because it's RIGHT THERE (visual), it's difficult for me to ignore and do a poor job maintaining these vehicles.

Often we will build a shadow board to stabilize so we know where things go. A shadow board is a board that has outlines of the tools on it, sort of like a parking lot for tools except, unlike a parking lot where cars park at many different angles, on a shadow board the tools can only go one way and you can easily see when one is missing. Picture an outline of a wrench on a board. When the wrench isn't hanging on the hook, you see

Got your Lean Lenses on?

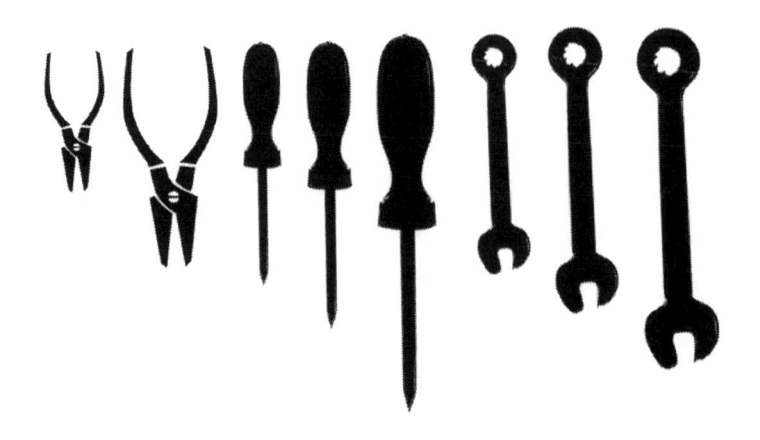

A Shadowboard done well makes it easy to see what's missing at just a glance!

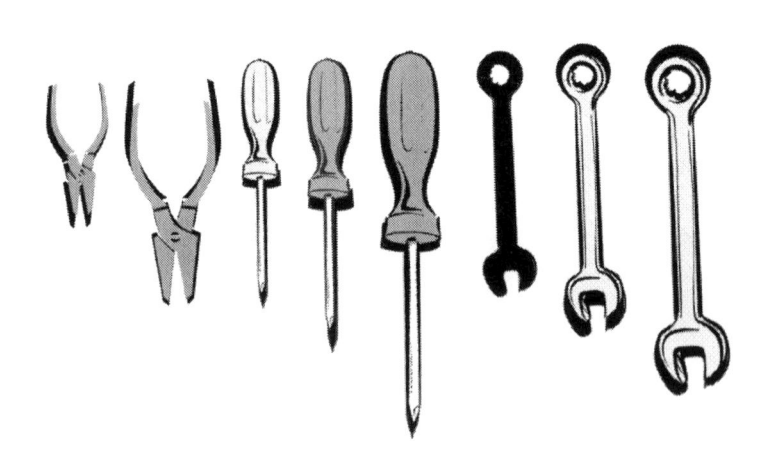

Got your Lean Lenses on?

that bright yellow wrench outline jumping out at you.

A shadow board done well makes it easy to see when something is missing or not in the right spot. Imagine pulling away from a gas pump but instead of putting the pump handle back onto its slot, you lay it on the ground. A gas pump holder is a great example of a shadow board. It's easy to use, there's really only one way to put the handle back and you can tell when it's not used correctly.

2: Stabilize

Organize the area so items are most convenient and easy to reach and use for the person working in the area (known as the process owner).

Building a cabinet nine feet high with tools on the top shelf for a five foot two process owner would be an example of what not to do!

Got your Lean Lenses on?

Shine

Shine means what it says, clean it up. It's Rudy Giuliani's broken window theory at work; people will keep a work area clean if it's clean and don't mind messing it up when it isn't.

But shine? What is shine? Sometimes it means painting the area, sometimes it just means scrubbing it down and getting rid of all the junk that has accumulated over time.

Shine does not mean making it look brand new again, which is confusing for some who mistakenly believe a plant must look like a showroom 24 hours per day. A clean, well ordered facility often has bumps & bruises; it doesn't need to be perfect.

When we shine up an area, it is easy to see what's happened; there might be a shadow board to make regularly used tools accessible. There will be a spot or two for garbage & recyclables so we intuitively understand how the area should work. And it will be clean.

3: Shine

Clean the work area and all equipment within it.

Got your Lean Lenses on?

Standardize

Imagine a row of cash registers in a grocery store. Each station has the cash register in the same place, the small bulletin board cashiers use for specials and the like in the same spot. Standardizing means we make similar work stations or processes alike so as we move people in & out of each of the areas the work they do is of the same high quality.

I have a friend who works in a manufacturing business that specializes in assembly of custom products of a similar type. The people who work in assembly are constantly frustrated by the salespeople who all write up their orders in their own style. How frustrating is that? Every time they receive an order from their salespeople they spend precious assembly time decoding a different salesperson's writing! The assemblers told my friend that they believed they were spending more than an hour everyday decoding all the information that arrived in different order /style.

After an evening telling stories sitting around motorcycles, I convinced my friend to get their salespeople together with the assembly folks to design one way, to standardize how the salespeople wrote up their orders. Once they did this, their mistakes immediately went down and productivity went up. It's our job (you and I) to help change minds around so we all think about the best way to standardize our processes rather than have the haphazard way we operate now.

Got your Lean Lenses on?

4: Standardize

Everything you can!

Standardized work areas make it easy to remain flexible with people, equipment and work!

Sustain

So now you have a work area that is clean, well organized, and intuitive to use for the worker who works there. It is a pleasure to work in and around. The challenge is keeping it that way. It's not impossible, but things won't stay that way unless we purposefully work at keeping it clean and improved.

Direct supervisors and managers are key players in keeping any improved area improved. Following up, MBWA (managing by walking around), and auditing an area will help the drive to sustain any 5S or improvement made. A monthly walk through with an audit form, a supervisor and a process owner helps to keeping an area sustained. An audit form should be as simple as possible, a basic excel form works just fine.

A Lean expert I know, Paul Douglas, has a great line I love to steal, "the only way to sustain an improvement is to improve upon it." When we do that we're able to call it continuous improvement, which is our real goal.

5: Sustain

The most difficult 'S' is always sustain, but hasn't that always been the case?

5-Why Fishbone Diagram (Ishikawa Diagram)

We use this to discover root causes of problems and identify relationships between causes and effects. What I appreciate about this tool is how simple and effective it is. Just by reviewing the example here, you will be an expert in how to use it.

First doodle out the fishbone, label the key areas of its skeleton manpower, machinery, methods, materials, environment or measurement (see diagram). One of these areas will likely represent the area the problem stems from.

Once you've got your fish, you can either write out or simply state what the problem is; 'the orders are being delivered late', then take your best guess at answering why the orders are being delivered late? Perhaps it's because a piece of equipment or machinery broke down. Why did the machine break? We had someone operate it that wasn't properly trained. Why wasn't he properly trained? We thought he knew what he was doing. Why did you think he knew what he was doing? Well, we didn't really know, we just guessed.

So you can see the order of events here:

1. Draw out your fishbone diagram.
2. List your problem.
3. Ask Why?
4. Answer question beginning at one of the 'bones', manpower, machinery, methods,

Got your Lean Lenses on?

5 Why Fishbone Diagram

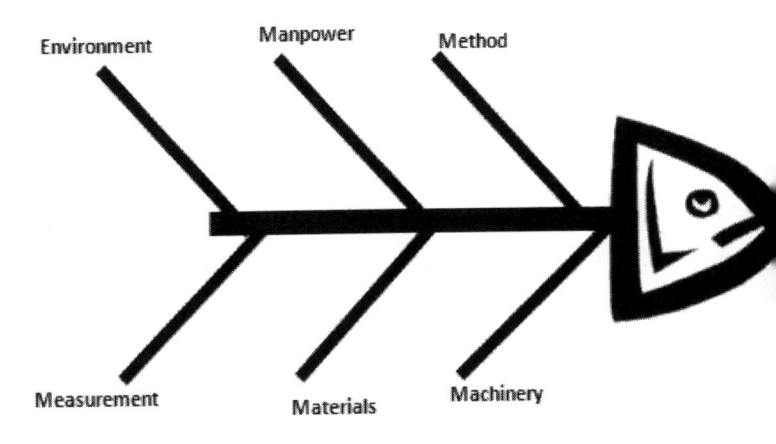

Got your Lean Lenses on?

materials, environment or measurement.

5. Ask Why?
6. Answer again.
7. Ask Why?
8. Answer again.
9. Repeat at least five times

Sometimes when you're asking why you will discover you have a couple bones going for the same issue. Good stuff, we want to get all of the potential issues on the table! If you back up, move to another bone and restart that's just fine. Like all tools, the more you use the more proficient you'll become.

It is always our goal with the fishbone to get to the 'system problem'. The system problem in our above example might be that we routinely accept guesses as real information or that we don't have training or check sheets in front of the piece of equipment.

Spaghetti Diagram

One of the best tools for removing waste is a spaghetti diagram, which ends up looking a lot like it sounds. It is extremely simple to use and just as effective.

We use this tool either by doodling or printing a map of the work area you're focused on, then spending time observing what's happening, and while you do so tracing out the person's steps as s/he performs their regular duties in that work area. On the next page you

Spaghetti Diagram Round 1:

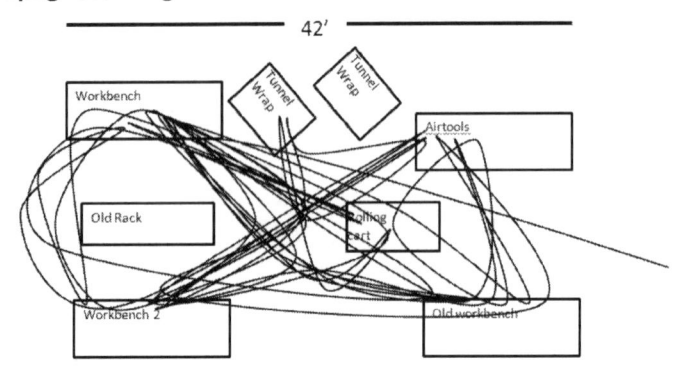

Have you got your 'Lean Lenses' on?
1. Are the benches disorganized?
2. Why is the old rack & old workbench there?
3. Why does he have to walk so far?

Spaghetti Diagram Round 2:

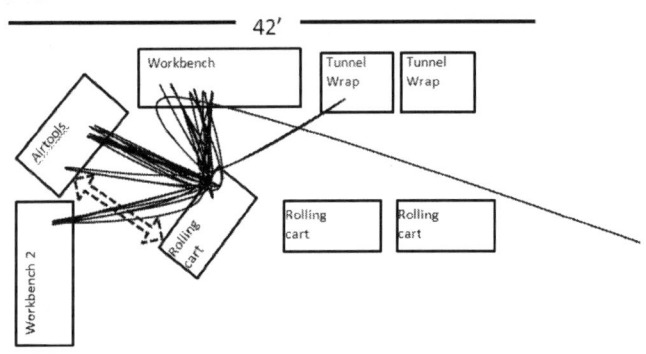

Have you got your 'Lean Lenses' on?
1. The work area has been 5S'd and is much smaller.
2. Very little walking to complete the work.
3. Inbound work now on rolling carts.

Got your Lean Lenses on?

see an example of a work area drawn out, and then someone has followed the worker as described, tracing out the route with all the stops and steps as he works. You can see that there is quite a bit of motion. Using the spaghetti chart helps you easily see where to relocate your tools and benches to minimize the waste of motion. When you can minimize motion you create a lot of time, don't you? You create time to produce more, or to produce faster, or you create time to add value somewhere else. You can see the changes happen over these few example pages; the small changes make big improvements simply rearranging the work area. Using the spaghetti diagram helps make improvements very easily.

Of course it's very easy to do this in a diagram, maybe not as easy in real life in your work area or office. Or is it? Using a spaghetti diagram only one time illustrates very easily that we can make work easier to do and more efficient. I've used this tool hundreds of times and it has never failed to reveal many issues within a work area.

There are so many options to rearrange; in our example we removed some old workbenches and tools. We 5S'd the tool bench to only keep the tools required. Then we rearranged the space itself, because the way this work is done we created a small work cell so it had a natural corner so the worker could reach each of the required items more easily.

Got your Lean Lenses on?

Spaghetti Diagram Round 3:

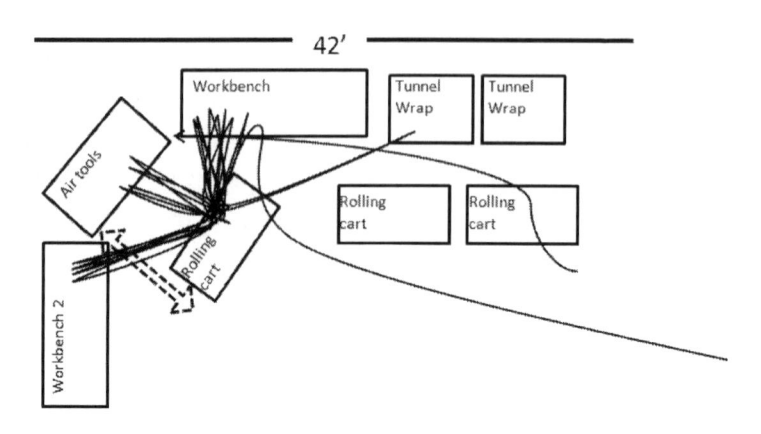

Reducing space available for work often makes it simpler and easier to complete by reducing many of the wastes without having to work hard to realize the gains!

Got your Lean Lenses on?

We also put the work onto rolling carts so the work could be easily moved into and out of the work area. Then we trained the worker to pull his cart closer to his bench (notice the dotted arrow) so he could reduce motion even further. So, many small improvements make this work area way more efficient while making the work easier to do, wins all around!

Cycle Time Reduction

Cycle time reduction is the process of reducing the time it takes to do any process. A process is defined as a series of steps to move or transform something from *a* to *b*. It could be the assembly of a number of parts into a single unit or the creation of a sales order and pick list from a customer email.

Most processes follow a series of set (or set in stone) steps that individuals follow time after time to achieve the desired result. When I get to Starbucks and order my Long Pour Grande Americano each morning the steps are set in motion and plus or minus they are the same in any of the hundreds of Starbucks I have visited over the last few years.

Cycle time reduction happens by following a series of simple, never changing steps:

Cycle Time Reduction is the method of reducing the time it takes to do any process.

1. Create a value stream map of each step in the process using post it notes.
2. Time each step at least three times to discover a best & worst time for each step.
3. Determine inputs & outputs for each step.
4. Highlight value added & non value added steps.
5. List issues from each step.
6. Remove waste from the process.
7. Create new value stream including standard operating procedure.

Each of the above steps by themselves are indeed quite simple. When we look at them all at once and try to visualize how they go together, it gets a bit complicated. Perhaps that's why when we work on projects people will often shortcut steps only to find that after a period of time they have to either start over or circle back to a prior step and begin again.

Trust me, there is no shortcut. Each time we work at cycle time reduction we must give each of the steps their due or we'll have to go back...
What's great about this tool is that it works every single time. What might be a bit tougher is walking you through how to do it in a book. The best way to learn is to learn by doing.

Got your Lean Lenses on?

Cycle Time Reduction Example:

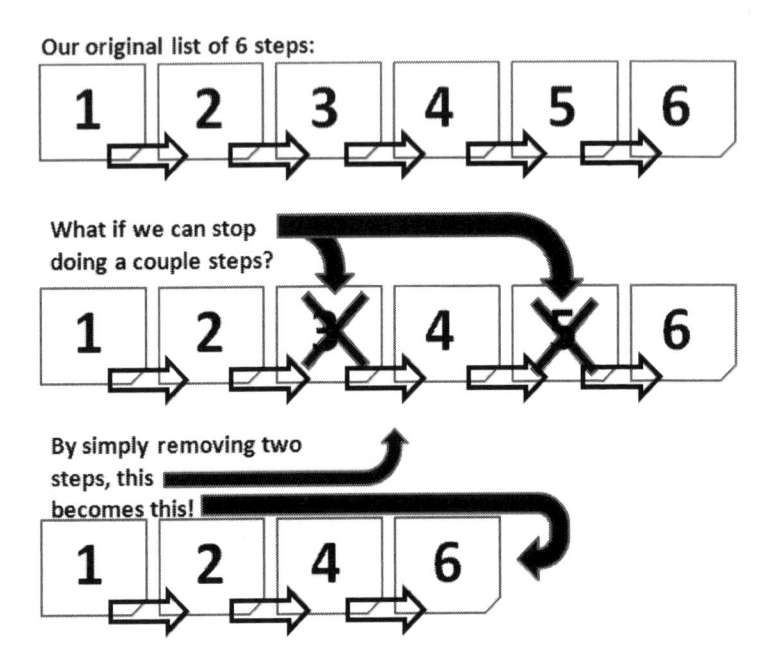

Our original list of 6 steps:

| 1 | 2 | 3 | 4 | 5 | 6 |

What if we can stop doing a couple steps?

| 1 | 2 | ✗ | 4 | ✗ | 6 |

By simply removing two steps, this becomes this!

| 1 | 2 | 4 | 6 |

Is it really this simple? Yes – only do *absolutely necessary* steps!

Got your Lean Lenses on?

Process Selection

Before we can do Cycle Time Reduction (CTR) we must first pick a process to do CTR on! The best projects to pick are bottlenecks or areas in your business that are problematic. For most of us there are a number of areas to pick from, particularly when you and your business are new to Lean.

Over time, project selection becomes more strategic, but for now we want to pick a process that we can be successful with.

For the example we walk through here, we'll try one we can pretty much all relate to, the Saturday morning grocery trip. We'll go through my Saturday morning grocery ritual with the goal of removing all (or as much as we can!) the waste and ending up with only the value added steps in the process. As a reminder, we define value as – something the customer is willing to pay for. In this process the customer is my wife.

Got your Lean Lenses on?

Cycle Time Reduction & Value Stream Mapping

Tools Required! Marker, Post-it Notes

Before you begin

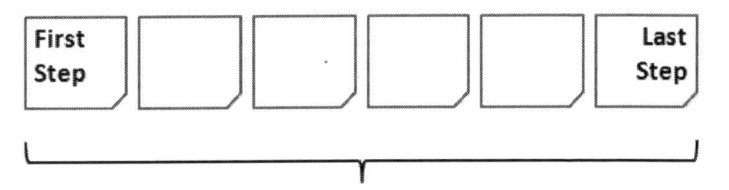

| First Step | | | | | Last Step |

Determine start and end scope of process to work on

Step 1

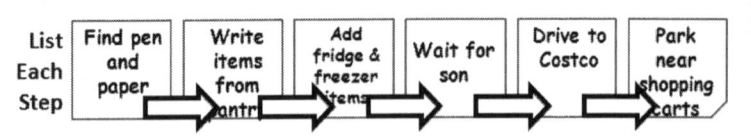

List Each Step → Find pen and paper → Write items from pantry → Add fridge & freezer items → Wait for son → Drive to Costco → Park near shopping carts

- Begin with first step, then step by step
  - Waiting is *always* an individual step – no exceptions
  - No steps should be left out

Got your Lean Lenses on?

Step 1

Create a value stream map (see opposite page) of each step in the process using post it notes.

Process: Saturday Morning Grocery Shopping

On the opposite page I've placed what the grocery trip process looks like on post it notes. It looks like this: Grab the running grocery list off the fridge, paper and pen, walk to fridge, open freezer, have a look, is there anything missing? Walk over to the spice cupboard, open it up, and realize I have no clue. On to the next cupboard, and so on. Walk to the upstairs pantry, peer in for anything we might need, go to the downstairs pantry, have a look, write a few items down, go into the laundry room and check the few things there. Then it's into the garage to check the freezer. Oh, back upstairs to ask my kids if they can think of anything, 'cereal, juice, ice cream'. As long as my son is ready to go, he & I are ready for our trip.

Once in the car we head to Costco, grab a cart and wait by the front door for them to open. Downside of leaving early, waiting with all the other early risers! Once all our shopping is completed we line up at the till, and wait for the checkout to begin. It's a busy morning at Costco so we wait for some time before beginning our checkout session.

Got your Lean Lenses on?

Step 2

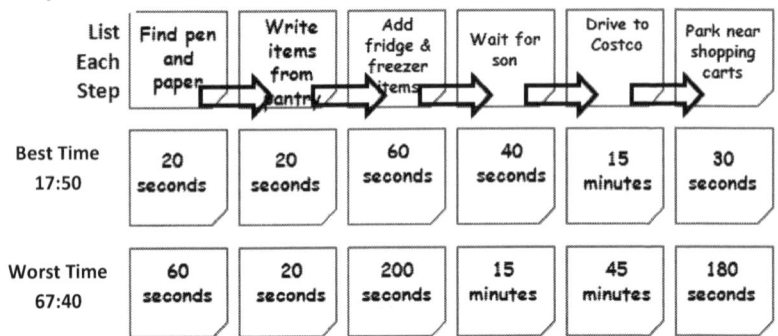

List Each Step	Find pen and paper	Write items from pantry	Add fridge & freezer items	Wait for son	Drive to Costco	Park near shopping carts
Best Time 17:50	20 seconds	20 seconds	60 seconds	40 seconds	15 minutes	30 seconds
Worst Time 67:40	60 seconds	20 seconds	200 seconds	15 minutes	45 minutes	180 seconds

- Time each individual step 3-4 times
  - Waiting is *always* an individual step – *no exceptions!*
  - No steps should be left out

Step 3

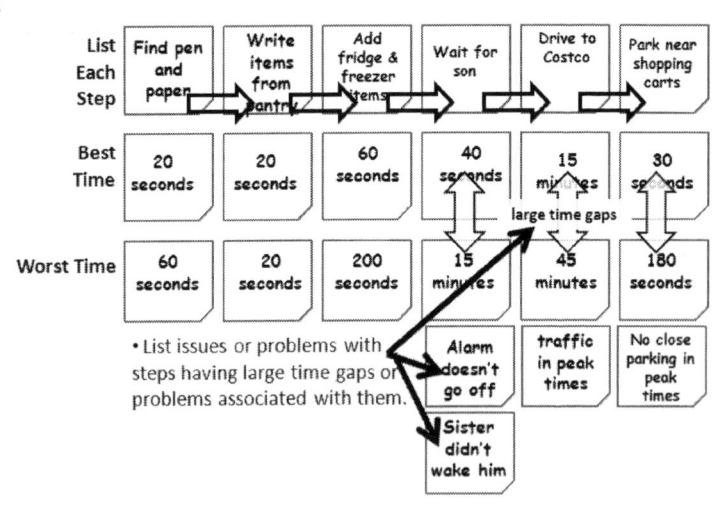

List Each Step	Find pen and paper	Write items from pantry	Add fridge & freezer items	Wait for son	Drive to Costco	Park near shopping carts
Best Time	20 seconds	20 seconds	60 seconds	40 seconds	15 minutes	30 seconds
					large time gaps	
Worst Time	60 seconds	20 seconds	200 seconds	15 minutes	45 minutes	180 seconds
				Alarm doesn't go off / Sister didn't wake him	traffic in peak times	No close parking in peak times

- List issues or problems with steps having large time gaps or problems associated with them.

Got your Lean Lenses on?

From there we drive three or four clicks to the local Save-On Foods. We repeat the process, only this time we don't get a buggy but one of those little green baskets. We proceed to the self checkout counter, wait in line, and then do our own self checkout. We pay then head back to the car for the short drive home.

I back in near the garage so it's a short walk to the pantry to put away the trunk full of stuff I've just purchased. I enlist some help from my kids to put groceries away but it is still more than half a dozen trips to the pantry, *anything to NOT take the oversized boxes Costco forces on its members! (I don't know this to be true, and I imagine that somewhere along the way the folks at Costco determined that if they gave their customers the boxes to take home they would reduce their recycling costs)*

Step 2

Time each step at least three times to discover a best & worst time for each step.

You can see (on the opposite page) I've timed the best and worst time for each step in my process. This example isn't the best for timing, but as long as you get the idea you can see why you will time things in your process!

Got your Lean Lenses on?

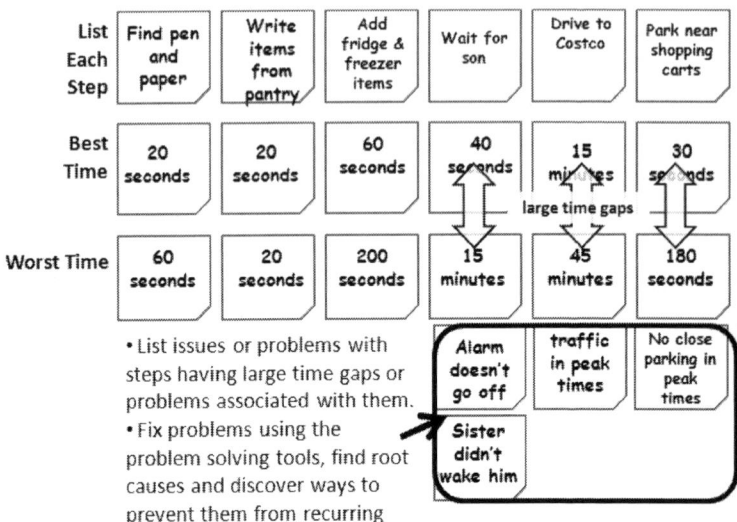

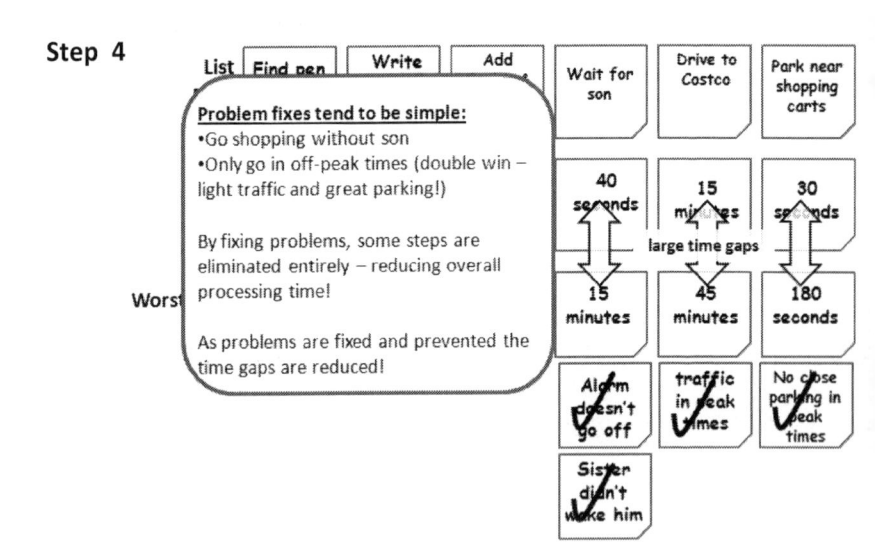

Step 3

List Each Step	Find pen and paper	Write items from pantry	Add fridge & freezer items	Wait for son	Drive to Costco	Park near shopping carts
Best Time	20 seconds	20 seconds	60 seconds	40 seconds	15 minutes	30 seconds
Worst Time	60 seconds	20 seconds	200 seconds	15 minutes	45 minutes	180 seconds

large time gaps

- List issues or problems with steps having large time gaps or problems associated with them.
- Fix problems using the problem solving tools, find root causes and discover ways to prevent them from recurring

- Alarm doesn't go off
- Sister didn't wake him
- traffic in peak times
- No close parking in peak times

Step 4

List	Find pen	Write	Add	Wait for son	Drive to Costco	Park near shopping carts

Problem fixes tend to be simple:
- Go shopping without son
- Only go in off-peak times (double win – light traffic and great parking!)

By fixing problems, some steps are eliminated entirely – reducing overall processing time!

As problems are fixed and prevented the time gaps are reduced!

40 seconds — 15 minutes — 30 seconds

large time gaps

15 minutes — 45 minutes — 180 seconds

- Alarm doesn't go off ✓
- Sister didn't wake him ✓
- traffic in peak times ✓
- No close parking in peak times ✓

Got your Lean Lenses on?

Step 3

List issues from each step.
For each of the steps we then list issues, or problems, associated with the step. We want to discover as many issues as we can with the steps, because we can't work at solving these issues or problems without knowing what they are. It won't surprise you that often we think we know what the problems are but once we start digging into something, we discover more or different problems than we had originally imagined.

Some examples of problems that are often discovered are things like not enough information is available to do the job or perhaps the component parts haven't arrived yet so the machine cannot be assembled.

One of the problems I had in my shopping process a couple of years ago was that not all the items wanted were on the fridge list, even though someone knew the items were needed. I corrected this problem by always doing my own checking. Shortly after I began creating my own list, my family simply stopped writing things down on the fridge list. Do you see the problem I created for myself? Now I write my own list because no one else will.

Got your Lean Lenses on?

Step 4

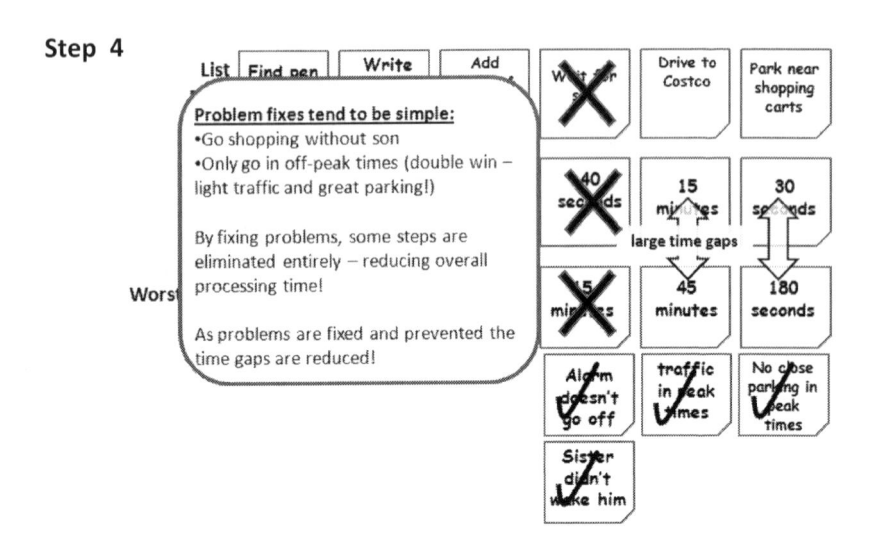

Problem fixes tend to be simple:
- Go shopping without son
- Only go in off-peak times (double win – light traffic and great parking!)

By fixing problems, some steps are eliminated entirely – reducing overall processing time!

As problems are fixed and prevented the time gaps are reduced!

Simple Results

Savings of over 42 minutes!

Best Time 17:10

Worst Time 25:20

Got your Lean Lenses on?

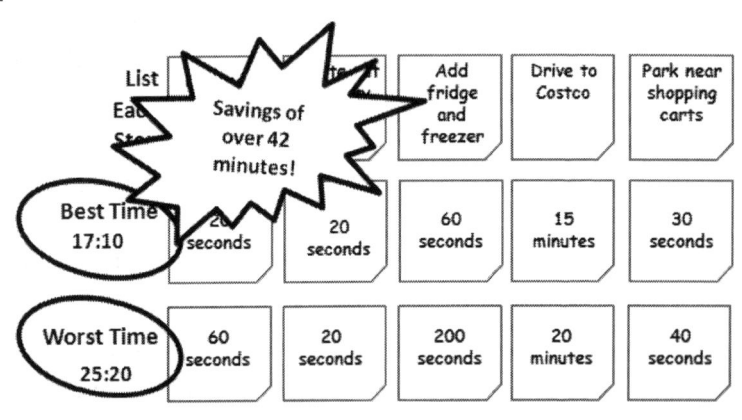

Step 4

Remove waste from the process.

Step four is to remove waste from the process, and by that we mean remove as much waste as you possibly can from the entire process.

This is a fairly easy thing to do, relatively speaking. As you work your way down the value stream map, you see a number of items that are non value added, can you simply stop doing them? That would be ideal, wouldn't it? In my shopping example I saved over 40 minutes per trip just by not bringing my son. I'm not saying my son is non-value added, but by not bringing him I save half an hour! In this case everyone wins as he hasn't been thrilled about coming with me for years.

Of course this is a simplistic example, just to illustrate what the process looks like. When you go through value stream mapping two or three times you'll see that there will be a good number of things you can simply stop doing. You won't mind, your customer won't notice, and your co-workers will be happy to not do things they knew were crazy anyway!

I worked in a business where every single day after the products were shipped, the accounting team billed the customers; then they would separate all the customer packing slips first alphabetically, and then by customer.

Got your Lean Lenses on?

Value Stream Mapping is a simple way to visually see all the steps required to complete any process!

Then they would take them over to the file cabinet and sort through and file them in the appropriate customer file. Then we did some value stream mapping.

We realized that the whole sorting by customer, separating tickets etc. was non-value added (for the customer, of course!); it took the ladies there about 35 minutes every day to do this task. We used our fishbone diagram as well as our spaghetti graph. We thought that maybe we could file by ship date. So we checked with the head office accounting people, and after they voiced some of their concerns they agreed we could try it out. When they agreed we could try it out I said, "Great! We've been doing it for two months already!" This business had thirty divisions all filing the same way. Let's do the math; 30 divisions X 0.5 hours/day X 260 business days per year X $15/hour = $58,500 saved. Every year.

Funny thing about that example? It took us months to get other divisions in the same company to agree to *try doing less work!*

In addition to items that are non-value added, check the steps where the best time and worst time steps have big gaps, you'll see spots where the best time is five minutes, and the worst time is thirty-five minutes (you'll see that spread and worse, trust me).

Got your Lean Lenses on?

Learning

is most

effective

when

it's fun.

Peter Kline
The Everyday Genius

Got your Lean Lenses on?

Why is the gap so large? When you start digging into the fishbone you'll find the most amazing things. Had to look for a wrench (hello shadowboard!), didn't have a pen, you name it you'll find it. John Shook tells a story in 'Becoming Lean' about when he was training in Japan in about 1984 where some of his American colleagues were so impressed with Toyota and Japan in general because in Japan it was why, why, why, and in North America it was who, who, who?

It's key when you are working at improving any project to focus on the process and avoid like the plague the temptation to blame the workers or anyone who helped set up the existing system. Always keep your mindset in the no blame mode.

Back to the value stream map. As you work the best time worst time angle, you'll see many issues that can be solved right away. Do that.

You will change the value stream around, stop doing some things, create shadow boards where the necessary tools are used. Perhaps you will add a control point upstream (don't bring all the parts to the assembly area unless we have all the parts), the possibilities are literally endless.

Our goal with the value stream is to remove as much waste as possible, and as you can imagine with my shopping trip the waste is plentiful.

Got your Lean Lenses on?

Lean is learning by doing!

20% training.

80% doing.

Got your Lean Lenses on?

How should I personally use these tools?

Earlier we covered amazingly simple yet powerful tools that we use as the basis of Lean. Each of us generally fits into either the employee or manager/owner category with the work we do each day.

The next few pages provide you with some things to consider as you work at implementing Lean in and around your business and life. It would be wise to read both sections, as it's good to understand where those around you are coming from.

Employee Role

The employee role in Lean is quite simple, participate. There isn't a much better feeling to be had at work than the feeling of making an improvement on an existing process or condition. An employee should participate and care simply for the rush that comes with making their work better.

How does the employee do that?

Got your Lean Lenses on?

Lean moves us from

"There's **no way** we can do that"

to...

"I'm **blown away** we did that!"

Get and remain curious about Lean. Work your customer and what they value, then repeat and never stop! To begin, learn about the eight wastes, and look for them in your job, ponder why they're there and look for ways to eliminate them. Use the wonderfully simple tools we have to remove waste.

Learn and do the 5S's, learn about root cause analysis (Ichikawa Diagram), learn about the spaghetti chart to doodle out processes and follow them from start to finish.

We've all heard about the concept of 80/20. Richard Koch, in his book entitled The 80/20 Principle, gives many terrific examples, including these easy to relate to ones; 20 percent of the people cause 80 percent of the problems, or 80 percent of the wear is done on 20 percent of a carpet and so on. Using the 80/20 rule and putting data into simple excel sheets can be very helpful in finding the right things to work on to remove waste. Talk to your customer to find out what they value and what they don't value, then focus your efforts on providing value.

I fondly remember asking one of my biggest customers what he valued about dealing with us.

Got your Lean Lenses on?

Only do things that are

'absolutely critical to the success of the business!'

He looked dumbfounded because he had never ever thought about it. When you ask your customers, some of their answers may surprise you. I recall being disappointed, he hadn't thought of what he valued about us (of course in reality it was our fault we hadn't helped him figure out what to value about us!)

A salesperson gets told thousands of time every year that a customer isn't buying because the price is too high. If that were always the case nothing would ever be purchased, yet there are i-pads, i-pods and expensive muscle cars everywhere!

Another customer had a number of sales people in his organization who had English as a second language. They could speak it well enough, but both they and their customers didn't read it very well. Our sales team discovered at a Kaizen event that we weren't making it easy for them to sell to their customers because all of our sales literature was English only!

So we found someone who both spoke and wrote in their language (it happened to be Punjabi), and we had our key target product brochures translated into Punjabi. We had intended to place them on their displays in their stores so that at least the displays would speak to the customers in their mother tongue.

Got your Lean Lenses on?

We Learn

10% of what we read

20% of what we hear

30% of what we see

50% of what we see and hear

70% of what we say

90% of what we say and do

Vernon A. Magnesen
Quoted in 'Quantum Teaching'

Got your Lean Lenses on?

When we presented the brochures to our customer we were shocked when he told us he wanted hundreds of each one. He was so excited with what we did he wanted stacks so his sales people could sell our products!

By focusing on what our customers valued we were able to easily fulfill their wants.

So, as employees, once we know the eight wastes and the tools to identify and eliminate waste along with what our customers value, we simply need to repeat these things over and over. You've seen the great t-shirt that changes depending on your hobby, Ride, Sleep, Repeat. Skate, Sleep, Repeat. Drum, Sleep, Repeat. Eat, Sleep, Repeat.

Lean, Sleep, Repeat.

Focusing your efforts on reducing waste and adding value to your customer will help you be a better employee in your workplace, which in turn will help you become a Lean leader in your workplace. Teach others about the tools. Keep it light and fun and the people around you will not only get better at what they do, you will too!

Got your Lean Lenses on?

Two Minute Rule:

Whatever it is, whenever it is, if it will take two minutes or less, do it immediately.

David Allen
Getting Things Done

Got your Lean Lenses on?

Personal Lean

Here are a number of my absolute favorite personal productivity tips; Lean is all about productivity, right?

The Two Minute Rule

David Allen talks in his book Getting Things Done, about 'the two minute rule'. The two minute rule is unbelievably simple, almost ridiculously so, but it simply states that whatever it is, if it takes two minutes or less, do it when you think about it, regardless of what it is or when it is. For example, if it's an e-mail you wanted to write and it'll take less than two minutes, do it when you think about it. At home it's bringing the recycling out, shredding some paper or checking the tire pressure of your wife's tires, doesn't matter what the task is (or wherever it hits you).

The two minute rule is magic. I've taught it to many people and many of them have come back to me over time and said, "It helps me have enough time for the bigger things I always have going on."

Sometimes I think the two minute rule was created by Albert Einstein when he said "make things as simple as possible, but not simpler."

The beauty of the rule is that as you do it over and over again, you train yourself to be action oriented, and stuff simply refuses to pile up; or at least when it does, it's because you intend it to.

A 'stop doing list' will immediately create more time for you.

Never go empty handed

This is self explanatory; whenever you go somewhere, whether you're walking, driving, or flying; stack up your reasons for where you're going and ask yourself, 'since I am going there anyway, what else can I bring along?'

I sort of wish my son would adopt this rule. I was in his bedroom the other day and there were four glasses all half full of water on his bedside table, yuck. I wonder if he knows, at 3:00 am, which one is the fresh one.

At the office there are many opportunities for this one aren't there? Walking to a printer, to the warehouse or plant; it's easy to stack tasks, if you put some thought into it.

Stop Doing List

We often think everything we do is necessary, or important to do. It's just not true. (Sorry).

Years ago a colorful fellow I worked for taught me to get and always keep a 'stop doing list' going. I was very busy, working full time and then working another 30 hours a week on my hobby, plus sports.

A 'stop doing list' can include many things, personal and work related. What kinds of things would you put on your stop doing list? Perhaps things like these: checking e-mail constantly, leaving your cell phone on all the time, treating all customers the same, doing everything

Make things
as simple
as possible,
but not simpler.

Albert Einstein

Got your Lean Lenses on?

your boss asks. The list of things to stop doing is absolutely endless!

Just Say No

With exercise and sports, Nike has it right, just do it. With personal efficiency, it's more like the other way around, just say no.

We all get way more offers than we could ever handle; my Mom taught me many years ago to be very picky to what I say yes to. Just this morning I was at a pancake breakfast my daughter was volunteering at and an older gentlemen put the touch on me to get involved in his favorite charity. Thankfully, I have been practicing saying no gracefully for years so when I left with my daughter I didn't bring some extra work (that was someone else's!) home.

When asked to do something or go somewhere, always begin (at least in your head) by answering no. It's far easier to turn a no to a yes than it is to turn a yes into a no.

Got your Lean Lenses on?

Management's Role is to ensure Deming's cycle of PDCA

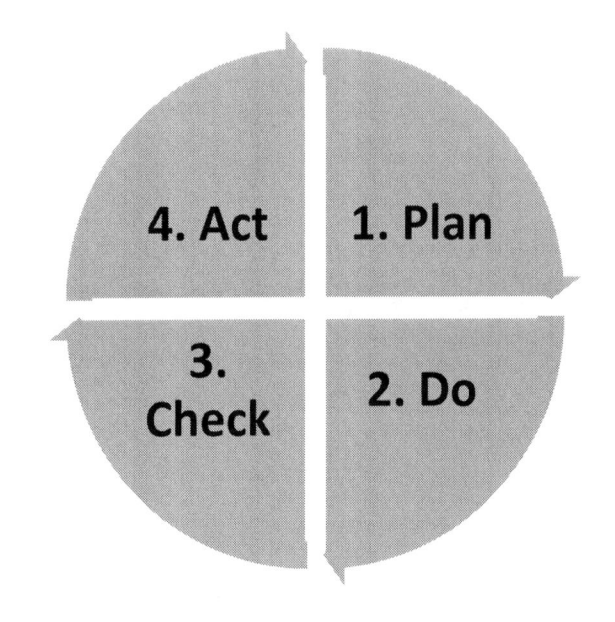

- 4. Act
- 1. Plan
- 3. Check
- 2. Do

is repeated over and over – *forever!*

Management Role

I had a mentor when I was a young sales rep, David Toews. David loved to tell stories and teach through conversations. He passed away when he was still a relatively young man but had coached many people to success in their careers. He loved to poke fun at himself and one story he told me more than once was, "in the seventies it was my job as the manager to tell people what to do and how to do it, now that we're in the nineties (circa 1997) it's my job to get out of their way and let them do what they want to do."

He knew he had to find ways not only to help his people do their job but also to remove obstacles that stand in the way of them getting their job done.

David was a Lean thinker without using the language of Lean. He knew intuitively what the role of the Lean leader is. He set direction for his business, targeted activities for adding value, then coached and coaxed high performance out of his people.

Got your Lean Lenses on?

Lean is not just for manufacturing.

Sure it's for offices and operations, but it's **especially for sales**!

Stephen Hall
Moulding & Millwork

Set a 'True North' Direction

W. Edwards Deming's 'constancy of purpose' or '14 points' business philosophy do a terrific job of articulating what True North might be for a company. Toyota adopted a version of these in their company, labeled TPS (Toyota Production System).

Deming's 14 points

Deming's 14 points apply everywhere from small organizations to mega corporations. Even a small work group or team can adopt them successfully.

1. Create constancy of purpose toward improvement of both product and service with the aim to be competitive and stay in business while providing jobs.
2. Adopt the new philosophy. Management must awaken to the challenge, learn their responsibilities, and take on leadership for change.
3. Cease dependence on inspection to achieve quality. Eliminate the need for inspection on a mass basis by building quality into the product in the first place.
4. End the practice of awarding business on the basis of price tag. Instead, minimize total cost. Move towards a single supplier for any one item, on a long-term relationship of loyalty and trust.

Got your Lean Lenses on?

In recent years at Matsushita Electric employees have submitted about 6.5 million ideas annually.

Toshihiko Yamashita
The Panasonic Way

5. Improve constantly and forever the system of production and service, to improve quality and productivity, and thus constantly decrease costs.
6. Institute training on the job.
7. Institute leadership. The aim of supervision should be to help people and machines do a better job. Supervision of management is in need of an overhaul, as well as supervision of production workers.
8. Drive out fear so that everyone may work effectively for the company.
9. Break down barriers between departments. People in research, design, sales, and production must work as a team, to foresee problems of production and other areas that may be encountered with the product or service.
10. Eliminate slogans, exhortations, and targets for the workforce asking for zero defects and new levels of productivity. Such exhortations only create adversarial relationships, as the bulk of the causes of low quality and low productivity belong to the system and thus lie beyond the power of the work force.
11. a. Eliminate work standards (quotas) on the factory floor. Substitute leadership.
b. Eliminate management by objective. Eliminate management by numbers, numerical goals. Substitute leadership.

Got your Lean Lenses on?

The only way to sustain an improvement is to improve upon it!

Paul Douglas
Moulding & Millwork

Got your Lean Lenses on?

12. a. Remove barriers that rob the paid worker of his right to pride in workmanship. The responsibility of supervisors must be changed from sheer numbers to quality.
b. Remove barriers that rob people in management and engineering of their right to pride in workmanship.
13. Institute a vigorous program of education and self-improvement.
14. Put everyone in the company to work to accomplish the transformation. The transformation is everyone's job.

Target Lean Activities for Leverage

Managers and leaders need to be specific about the activities they target around Lean by selecting activities that will truly leverage each area of the business's strengths.

Deming noted in the 1950's that problems were caused 80% of the time by the systems companies have in place and 20% by the people working them. In his later years he revised those numbers to 96% of problems coming from systems and 4% caused by the people working in them. I've learned over the years he was absolutely correct.

Got your Lean Lenses on?

Business A –
excels with Lean.

Business B –
plods, why?

Think 50%

Got your Lean Lenses on?

Our systems and processes seem to have been designed for the company's benefit, not the system users. When we design systems for the company's benefit instead of the user we tend not to think about what life will be like for that user. Often we don't really care what it's like to use the system. We say, 'just use it and stop asking questions', or, 'stop complaining and do your job'. How loony is that?

Coaching & Developing Their People
As Lean is 50% process and 50% people it means that the implementers of Lean, managers and supervisors, should spend about 50% of their available Lean time working directly with their people. What would they do while spending so much time with their people? They can do Kaizen, they can search for problems, coach for improvement, design work, the list is endless!

Keeping things light
Keeping business light is a key to being successful with Lean because people want to be inspired, not only once in a while, but regularly. Wouldn't it be terrific if going to work every day inspired you? It's certainly possible if you keep things light enough that the people who work with and for you enjoy themselves, and are able to improve their jobs.

Focus on the process.
When we're having a problem, any problem, focus on the process and move into problem solving mode.

Lean is 50% process and 50% people; guess which is the more important 50%?

Turn the page to see the answer!

Problem solving mode

Many of us are good problem solvers. However, a challenge is we tend to skip the steps of problem solving and go right to solution mode without truly understanding the problems we're trying to solve.

I was working with a colleague (same business, different division) on an inventory problem we were sharing (fortunately for me, it was more his problem than mine!) and in our small work group I really wanted to understand the problem. My colleague wasn't that interested in understanding the problem. He had spent time thinking about it prior to our meeting, I suppose, and had all the solutions worked out. I kept saying over and over, "I don't think we know enough about the problem." I was after detail and he only wanted to discuss his solutions. It won't surprise you that his solutions benefitted his divisions greatly but didn't do much to help mine (truly one-sided, it's-all-about-me thinking).

We were scheduled to work on the problem for two days and we hadn't been at it for more than an hour and my friend had already decided what the best solution should be. It was disheartening and disappointing because a colleague and I flew to this person's business with a real intention of working

Got your Lean Lenses on?

The important 50% is the people 50%.

Without people you won't need a process!

towards a solution that would benefit not only his divisions but ours as well. By jumping to the solution stage, my friend had turned his brain off not only to truly understanding the problem but also to working toward a mutually beneficial group of solutions!

50% Process and 50% People

In one facility we worked at, there was a fellow who had worked there for more than fifteen years. His name was Karl and he wasn't that excited about a bunch of suits coming into his area to tell him how to do his job. In his mind, not only did we not know his job, we sure weren't going to help him do it any better! We all know Karl, don't we? Anyway, we did the training in his area and trained him as well as those around him; he participated, but it was obvious to all that his heart wasn't in it. We kept at it and kept at it. Eighteen months later he delivered his first improvement idea. By then, the supervisors had learned to encourage those who came up with the ideas to go ahead and make the changes they suggested.

It took Karl a few days, but once he completed his improvement idea he was quite happy. The supervisor was happy that Karl was able to contribute, but those around Karl were VERY happy. They not so quietly teased and congratulated him on his idea. They wondered what had taken him so long, what's next, etc.

Got your Lean Lenses on?

Lean is bottom up and top down.

The bottom participates and the top directs, drives, and leads.

Of course it didn't take eighteen months for his next improvement idea, or his next or the one after that! Now he participates, brings improvement ideas and an outsider would likely not be able to guess who the latecomer is! We've all seen the graph that shows that with most initiatives driven by management there are 10% early adopters, 80% who just go along, and another 10% who'll 'wait and see'. Karl is simply a wait and see-er, he wanted to know that Lean wasn't going to go away like so many other initiatives he'd seen come and go over the years. Once he realized the business was in it for longer than the current manager would be, he decided he could be in it for the long haul as well.

Bottom up and top down

I've had a number of executives tell me they like Lean because it is a bottom up system rather than a top down one; not only do I not understand that comment, it's absolutely 100% incorrect. Nothing could be further from the truth. In reality, if a business wants to truly adopt Lean, the executives not only need to be involved, they need to be the key drivers if they are to get it into all the layers of the business. How will managers and supervisors underneath ownership and executive get their coaching? Why would managers coach and teach their people if no one is coaching them?

Lean

(Continuous Improvement)

can never end, the cycle continues forever as we strive to provide as much value as we possibly can for our customer.

It is easy to tell the difference between businesses implementing Lean when we walk through them. If the person in charge operates like a coach, Lean has a good chance of becoming part of the fabric. If the person is a top down manager (my way or the highway), Lean will die like so many flavor of the month fads. But Kevin, you just advocated that executives need to be involved and leading the charge and now you're saying that if the manager works a top down style it won't work. Yes, and both statements are correct; Lean is not an either/or proposition as it relates to management style, it's more a culture of let's work on our problems together than a do it like this style.

Lean needs top down participation in order to get bottom up participation. People today don't think of their employers like previous generations did; they've seen their parents and peers get let go while their bosses right size the business. Owners, executives, middle managers and supervisors all need to be involved to train the level of people below them, and those below them, so the vast majority of workers and employees not only buy in, but believe in and work at bringing Lean into their regular workday. It's hard for people to believe what they're being told; it's much easier for us to believe what we see.

Got your Lean Lenses on?

If you do not live in the future today, you will live in the past tomorrow.

Peter Ellyard
Executive Director, Preferred Futures,
of Australia

Got your Lean Lenses on?

Conclusion

Everywhere we go we see things we wish were different.

Lean thinking and problem solving tools can help us bring those things closer to where we'd like them to be. Change is not for the faint of heart but as you invest in thinking about value and customers and removing waste your life will continually get more interesting!

Enjoy your journey!

Got your Lean Lenses on?

Level One Lean Terms

Balanced production: A system where all operations produce at the same cycle time.

Bottleneck: Any work area or process that has a capacity less than the demand.

Changeover: The process of changing a machine or system from being setup to run product A to product B.

Continuous Flow Production: Single-piece or one-piece flow refers to a production process where product flows continuously, one piece at a time from step to step.

Current State Map: A map showing the current production process or system.

Cycle Time: The entire time to complete one cycle of an operation, from beginning to end.

Error Proofing: Designing mistakes or errors out of a process, thereby preventing errors. Also know as Poke Yoke.

Five S (5S): A system of keeping a work area in a clean well organized condition. It includes the following steps:

1: Sort
2: Stabilize
3: Shine
4: Standardize
5: Sustain

Flow: Think of flow like a stream or river, we want our systems to flow with very few rocks slowing the river or stream down.

Gemba: The place where the work gets done, it may be the shop floor, an office, or even a salesman's car.

Heijunka: Heijunka is leveling the workload whether it is production, shipping, receiving or any process.

Kaizen: A blend of Japanese words that mean small or good change.

Kaizen Blitz: A Kaizen Blitz describes a session wherein a group of people target a work area and make many small improvements (Kaizen) in a football 'blitz' attack style.

Lead Time: The entire time a customer waits to receive their product after placing an order.

Lean: A Business system or philosophy that utilizes a set of problem solving tools to help maximize value added for the customer while minimizing waste within the business system.

Got your Lean Lenses on?

Muda: Is the Japanese term for waste, see Waste.

Non-Value Added: Any activity or action that adds no value to the product or service which by nature makes them waste.

Overproduction: Producing more than is required by customer or the next process.

PDCA: Plan, Do, Check, Act. A cycle of problem solving that is repeated over and over to improve any system over time.

Poke-Yoke: Also know as error proofing or mistake proofing; used well poke yoke is designed into a system to help prevent errors.

Pull System: A pull system is one which only produces work when it is 'pulled' from the customer.

Sensei: Japanese for teacher.

Standard Work: Is a system of doing work in a standardized way so that regardless of who is doing it, the work is done the same way. Using standard work helps maintain consistent quality and workflow.

Takt Time: German term that means heartbeat, also known as the heartbeat of the customer. To calculate

Got your Lean Lenses on?

takt time we take the number of available minutes in a workday, divided by the number of units the customer requires. E.g. 480 minutes per day / 100 units = takt time of 4.8 minutes.

Value: Is defined as something the customer is willing to pay for. Only the customer can determine what they value.

Value Stream: A list of all the steps in order from the beginning of a process to the end of a process. Waiting must always be listed as an individual step.

Value Stream Mapping: Is the process of creating a Value Stream. Creating a value stream map can be done with pen & paper or a computer. The easiest and most effective way of Value Stream Mapping is using Post-it notes because it is very simple to do; it is visual, is easily changed and most people can 'get it' after only a single session.

Waste : Anything the customer is not willing to pay for.

Yokoten: Japanese word describing sharing practices everywhere, across businesses up and down the hierarchy so all are on the same plan.

Bibliography

Allen, D. *Getting Things Done.*
Ball, Sir C. *More Means Different*
Kline, P. *The Everyday Genius*
Koch, R. *The 80/20 Principle*
Liker, J *(Edited by) Becoming Lean*
Slater, R. *Jack Welch and the GE Way*
Vos, J. and Dryden, G. *The Learning Revolution*
Yamashita, T. *The Panasonic Way*

Got your Lean Lenses on?

Index

5S, 85, 87, 89, 91, 93, 95, 103, 131
5-Why, 105
80/20, 131
Acknowledgements, 169
Albert Einstein, 137, 140
Andrew McFadyen, 82
Becoming Lean, 127
Bob Low, 170
bottom up, 157, 159
broken window theory, 99
Bruce Hamilton, 34
coach, 151, 157, 159
continuous improvement, 103
Costco, 69, 117, 119
Cycle Time Reduction, 111, 114, 115
David Chao, 68, 170
David Toews, 143
Defects, 57, 59
Deming, 145, 149
Dryden, G., 166
eight wastes, 25, 27, 32, 75, 131, 135
employee, 129, 135
empty handed, 139
executive, 157
fishbone diagram, 105, 107, 125, 127
GBMP, 34
Getting Things Done, 137
Google, 23
How to use, 15
improvement, 103, 129, 145, 149, 151, 155
Ishikawa Diagram, 105
Jack Welch, 70, 166
Joey Higuchi, 170
John Shook, 64, 127
just say no, 141
Lean Sensei International, 68, 82, 170
managers, 103, 151, 157, 159
manufacturing, 63, 101
More Means Different, 50
motion, 31, 33, 35, 43, 49, 109, 111
Unnecessary motion, 31
Motion, 31
necessary waste, 79
Nike, 141
overproduction, 67
Overproduction, 67, 69
Paul Douglas, 103
Peter Ellyard, 160
Peter Kline, 126
processing, 37, 63, 65

Got your Lean Lenses on?

Processing, 63
productivity, 101, 137, 147
quality, 17, 21, 101, 145, 147, 149
Red Tag, 91
Richard Koch, 131
Rudy Giuliani, 99
Save-On Foods, 119
saving, 33, 53
shadow board, 95, 97, 99
Shigeo Shingo, 25, 71
shine, 99
Sir Christopher Ball, 50
sort, 89, 95, 125, 139
spaghetti diagram, 107, 109
spaghetti graph, 125
stabilize, 95
standardize, 101
Starbucks, 17, 35, 75, 111
Stephen Hall, 144
stop doing list, 139
storage, 49, 51, 53, 55
supervisors, 93, 103, 149, 151, 155, 157, 159
The eight wastes, 25

The Everyday Genius, 126
The Learning Revolution, 166
The Panasonic Way, 146, 166
top down, 157, 159
Toshihiko Yamashita, 146, 166
Toyota, 25, 127, 145
transportation, 43, 45, 47
Transportation, 43
True North, 145
two minute rule, 137
value, 17, 19, 21, 23, 27, 31, 47, 59, 61, 63, 65, 71, 73, 77, 85, 109, 113, 115, 117, 123, 125, 127, 131, 133, 135, 143
value stream map, 113, 117, 123, 125
Vernon A. Magnesen, 134
Vos, J, 166
waiting, 37, 39, 47, 49, 51, 59, 63, 117
Whole Foods, 21

Got your Lean Lenses on?

Acknowledgements

The body of knowledge around Lean is ever expanding and so much of it comes by doing. Of course, I've read many books about Lean and the famous authors like Liker, Hoseus, and Meier have had a major impact on me. Bringing their writings to life has been my sensei - David Chao (Lean Sensei International), coaching and challenging me freely. Thanks for your help and trading choice assignments for chocolate! David's team of coaches (Hilda Henry, Bob Low, Andrew McFadyen, and Joey Higuchi) are selfless first class teachers.

I've been very lucky to work with a terrific group of people at Sauder Industries Ltd. who've taught me so much; Rich McKerracher and so many peers and managers, all great to work with, thank you so much!

I've had lots of help with this book in the form of editing by my friend Kristin MacMillan and newly found daughter, Haley Radke, your advice and feedback has been terrific, thank you!

My family has been very patient with me for taking so much precious time to work at one Lean project or another over the last few years, thank you, especially Linda, easily the best wife I could have asked for!

About the Author

Kevin has been with Sauder Industries Ltd. for over twenty years; is a certified Lean Master Blackbelt, he has held various management roles with Sauder Industries Ltd., including managing various distribution businesses as well as developing and delivering both sales and branch management training programs. He has leadership experience in sales and operations; with this real world experience he easily relates to all levels within organizations and situations. Kevin has an insatiable appetite for reading with interests ranging from organizational behavior to Lean and process improvement.

Kevin appreciates teaching and speaking about Lean within Sauder Industries Ltd., as well as in public or private workshops, in addition to leading on-site kaizen events.

Kevin lives in Fort Langley, British Columbia, Canada, with his wife Linda and three great kids. His hobbies include motorcycling, reading, football, and hiking.

Kevin can be contacted at:
kevinw@mouldingandmillwork.com
wack01@telus.net
604-882-0434

Made in the USA
Middletown, DE
20 September 2018